I0816181

CENTERED

Seven Practices to Build Self-Awareness, Renew Confidence, and Discover Inner Peace

TINA HENDERSON

Centered: Seven Practices to Build Self-Awareness, Renew Confidence, and Discover Inner Peace

Published by Clovercroft Publishing, Franklin, Tennessee

Cover and Interior Design by Suzanne Lawing

Printed in the United States of America

ISBN: 978-1-956370-97-3 (print)

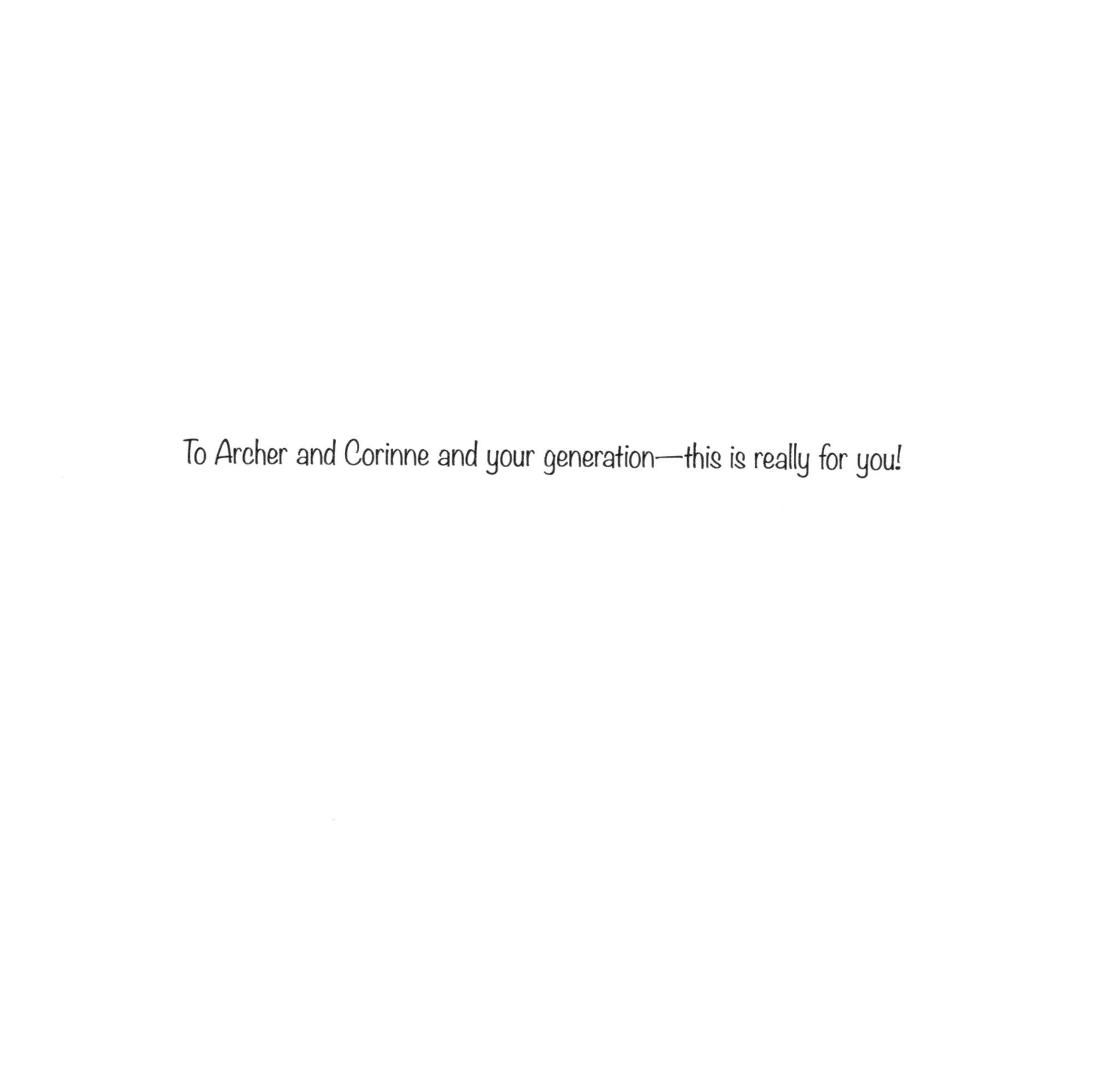

To Archer and Corinne and your generation—this is really for you!

~The most simple and basic way to empower yourself is through self-awareness and reflection~

INTRODUCTION

This book has been evolving for years—just like me.

For as long as I can remember, I've been drawn to offering inspiration, perspective—and encouragement—especially to young people. It's part of my DNA.

After decades of teaching adolescent girls and raising two strong, resilient daughters of my own, a vision began to take shape: I would write a book about what I knew best and felt most deeply about—empowering girls.

The premise was clear: by integrating a set of intentional, meaningful practices into their daily lives, girls could unlock deeper self-awareness, build confidence, and step into their strength. In essence, they could find their center.

As the years passed, the reality of life had its way of shifting my perspective. I navigated the emotional terrain of parenting young adults, mourned the loss of my father, adapted to the changing rhythms of aging and retirement, and held my daughter's cancer diagnosis close to my heart. Each experience shaped me and tested my resilience. The joy of becoming a grandparent, in particular, brought a profound sweetness to my life, adding a layer of purpose, grace and joy.

Through this journey, one truth became clear: the message I was writing wasn't just for girls; it was for all of us. *GirlCentered* became *Centered* because the practices that help young women thrive are the same ones that can guide anyone, at any stage of life, back to themselves.

You, Give, Care, Grow, Connect, Talk, and **Engage** are more than just habits: they are essential pathways to empowerment. They foster clarity, strength, and resilience. They invite you to believe in and trust yourself. They remind you that the answers you seek are already within you and that you are your own hero.

Practices

You

Give

Care

Grow

Connect

Talk

Engage

Trust

You

Strive to be your true, authentic self.

Discovering

and

embracing

who you really are takes time and courage.

ASK YOURSELF:

What do I really care about?

What matters to me?

What do I believe in?

What gets me out of bed in the morning?

As you uncover the real you,
share it with the world,
and present yourself in a way
that feels just right to you.

This journey takes time and involves trial and error.

Be humble, yet confident,
proud of who you are,
who you've unleashed,
and who you've become.

Don't waste your energy
trying to meet others' expectations.
You don't need to change
or conform.

Invest in being you.

Eventually, you'll feel more

CENTERED

and

REAL.

Remember.
There is only one YOU.

You are more than enough.

Give

Care about other people, and give to them.

Try to put yourself in their shoes,
imagining what they are going through.

Learn from those who are different from you.

Everyone has a lot to offer.

Everyone has **stuff**.

When we help and care for others, showing

understanding,

kindness, and

compassion,

we are connecting

and growing.

Over time, you will gain
a deeper understanding
of both the people
and the world around you,
while also learning more about yourself.

This process can be magical!

Care

It is more than ok to put yourself

first.

Caring for others adds so much value to our lives,
but taking care of YOU,
must be a priority as well.

When you care for yourself,
you build self-respect,
creating the space to
care for others more effectively.

Taking good and focused care of yourself,
allows you to see everyone
and everything else more clearly.

This practice does not have to be elaborate,
or overly time-consuming.

Start with small, lasting habits like:

getting good rest;
moving regularly to stay fit and strong;
nourishing your body well;
treating yourself with love and compassion,
as you would treat a best friend.

Find the time to tend to your own
needs,
feelings,
dreams,
and goals.

Regularly incorporating self-care into your life will leave you feeling
more energized,
stronger,
healthier,
more confident.

And centered.

Grow

Be curious.

Try new things.

Think outside the box.

Take chances.

You'll make mistakes.

Embrace them.

Fall
and
get
back
up.

Avoid the trap of trying to be PERFECT.

Perfection does not exist.

Instead, focus on making progress and doing the best you can.

Remind yourself:
you can't please everyone;
you can't do it all.

Ask for help when you need it.

You are human.

Through this practice, you will
learn and grow,
evolve,
and improve.

As you work through your setbacks
and acknowledge your imperfections,
you will gain resilience,
and perspective.

You will find your way back home.

Connect

Build meaningful connections with people who make you feel yourself, who:

encourage you,
believe in you,
listen to you,
respect you,
and love you.

Choose those who bring out the best in you and who lift you up.

Get involved.

Join.

Help out:

at your school,
in your neighborhood,
within your community,
inside your family.

Ask someone how their day is going.

Text a friend.

Call your mom!

When you improve and expand your attachments with others, you begin to see people and situations more clearly.

Your relationships become deeper and more effortless.

Your place of belonging will emerge.

Connection and **belonging** are important and essential parts of being

human.

When you sense that you belong, chances are you'll be able to

take on more,
feel more alive
and less alone,
and flourish.

You so deserve this.

Talk

Good communication includes expressing your

beliefs,
feelings,
and needs.

Equally important is creating space for others to do the same.

Communicating in today's world, however, is challenging.

There is so much excessive noise,
negativity,
distraction,
and technology
to hide behind.

Strive to be present and mindful
in your interactions.

Put your phone down,
especially when in the presence of others.

Participate in real, face-to-face conversations.

Listen well.
Truly hear other people's perspectives.

Be open to new ideas.

Ask questions.

The world is so colorful.

There is so much to learn.

Advocate for yourself, standing up for your beliefs.

Do so politely and thoughtfully and respectfully.

By learning to communicate effectively,
not only
will you feel
heard and valued,
you will also hear others more fully,
and ultimately arrive at a greater understanding of yourself.

This, too, will center you.

Engage

Find the time to do more of what you love,
that which brings you joy,
ignites you,
and takes you away from your everyday worries and concerns.

I love writing,
swimming,
taking long walks with friends,
skiing,
spending time with family,
and finding opportunities to laugh and smile.

Perhaps you enjoy
dancing
or practicing yoga,
singing or reading,
jumping rope or playing soccer,
painting or crocheting.

Whatever you love to do,
create the time
and space
to incorporate these activities into your life,
pursuing them with as much enthusiasm as you can.

Your focus and choices most likely will change over time.

That's ok.

Doing more of what you love,
will provide you with a sense of
MEANING and PURPOSE.
It will nourish your mind,
body and spirit,
and help you feel more
powerful and energized,
more balanced,
and, yes...
CENTERED.

What do you love spending your time doing?

I trust you'll have fun figuring it out.

Trust

You did it!

By staying true to yourself,
trusting your instincts,
focusing,
and noticing...
you have become your own
HERO
possessing unique strengths,
quirks,
originality and authenticity.

Congratulations.

You've clarified exactly who you are
and taught yourself
how to feel better.

This discovery can be truly transformative.

By integrating these simple practices into your life,
you are better equipped to

navigate the world more easily and confidently,

view yourself more completely and honestly,

and help others more often and readily.

You'll face challenges with greater confidence and resolve.

And you'll thrive.

Go ahead.
Look in the mirror and pat yourself on the back.

You have found your path,
your renewed trust in yourself,

your center.

The End

THANK YOU

Writing *Centered* has been a profoundly powerful experience for me in numerous ways. I have learned an enormous amount about others, and myself. I have improved my writing beyond what I thought possible. But, I could not have arrived here without the help of many.

My creativity was fueled by the love, support and patience of my family and friends. My children, Stephanie, Will and Emma, and son-in-law Austin, relentlessly made fun of how long it has taken me, and how I struggled so with technology, but they continuously championed me, urging me forward. They are my everything. My beloved grandchildren, Archer and Corinne, were my true inspiration. My desire for their generation to do, and be, better, propelled me over the finish line. To my parents, who grounded my values— I am forever grateful. To Jen, who always says the right thing, Andy, who always does the right thing, and Jon, who always writes the right thing— you three are my rocks. To Constance, who held my hand throughout this journey, in such a kind and supportive way, leading me back to myself— thank you.

And, finally, to my husband Paul— my entire world. Nothing would be the same, or as exciting, without you.